Christ Our Savior

The Greatest Prophecy

Isaiah 53

JOHN C. WHITCOMB

John C. Whitcomb

6/11/14

CHRIST OUR SAVIOR: THE GREATEST PROPHECY—ISAIAH 53

Whitcomb Ministries
Indianapolis, Indiana
whitcombministries.org

ISBN – 13: 978-0615980430

***

Thanks to my friends at the Institute for Creation Research, Dallas, Texas, who transcribed the audio lectures that formed the basis of this book.

CONTENTS

FOREWORD

This new book on Isaiah 53 by Dr. John C. Whitcomb is an exceptional exposition of this unparalleled prophecy of God's promised Messiah, which was delivered to the nation of Israel seven hundred years before Jesus Christ was born.

A significant feature of this book is Dr. Whitcomb's use of the original language of the biblical text of Isaiah 53 to shed light on the meaning of the prophecy. In addition, he rightly emphasizes the great significance of Isaiah's prophecy by pointing out that the New Testament authors of the books of Matthew, Mark, Luke, John, Acts, Romans, and 1 Peter all referred back to the Isaiah 53 passage to show that the Jesus Christ of their day was, in fact, the promised Messiah foretold in Isaiah.

The thing that made the greatest impact upon me while reading Dr. Whitcomb's book is the emphasis that it was Christ *alone* who endured the punishment for our sins while on the cross. Even His heavenly Father had to forsake Him during that time. If only for that emphasis, I think every person should read this book.

Renald E. Showers
Author and Speaker
Friends of Israel Gospel Ministry

❶

THE MYSTERY OF CHRIST

Isaiah 52:13-15

Of all the Old Testament prophecies of the coming Messiah, or Christ, none can quite compare to Isaiah's portrait of the Lord's Servant in Isaiah 53. Writing some seven hundred years before the birth of Jesus, the prophet described the rejection, death, and exaltation of Christ in such clear terms that almost everyone who reads these words immediately recognizes that they are describing the work of and response to the Lord Jesus Christ.

Introduction

For hundreds of years, the Spirit of God has been preparing men and women to appreciate the special beauty and significance of this supreme portrait of His beloved Son. As we look at this passage—which actually begins with an introductory section starting in Isaiah 52:13—let us consider the methods the Holy Spirit has used to focus our attention on this amazing portion of Scripture. In at least three ways, God has succeeded in drawing our attention uniquely to this prophecy.

First, He has done so through repeated *quotation* of the passage in the New Testament. This specific portion of Isaiah's prophecy is quoted directly in Matthew 8, Mark 15, Luke 22, John 12, Acts 8, Romans 10, Romans 15, and 1 Peter 2. The first six books of the New Testament, plus 1 Peter, are saying to us that if we really want to know who Jesus the Messiah is, if we really want to know who God's Son is and what He came to accomplish in this world, we need to go back to Isaiah 52–53.

The second method God has used to focus our attention on this passage is *location*. As the quotations bring us back to this passage in Isaiah, we are amazed to find its prominent and central location in the Old Testament. It is not tucked away in some obscure portion of the Old Testament Scripture but is found in the very heart of the greatest of the writing prophets—Isaiah, the Prince of the Prophets. And it is not tucked away in some obscure portion of Isaiah either. It is found in those last twenty-seven chapters of Isaiah, the "New Testament" portion that begins with the voice of one crying "in the wilderness" (40:3), a reference to John the Baptist (Matthew 3:1-3).

Furthermore, this messianic prophecy is not tucked away in some obscure portion of the final chapters of Isaiah. Those last twenty-seven chapters are divided beautifully into three groups of nine chapters each, and each of those nine-chapter sections has a special emphasis. Chapters 40–48 focus our attention on the imminent collapse of Israel's enemies, especially Babylon, which is symbolic of all satanic opposition. The central nine chapters, 49–57, focus on God's means of deliverance for Israel, namely, her personal Messiah. Then the final nine chapters of the book, 58–66, emphasize God's marvelous future for Israel during the kingdom age.

This great prophecy is found in the central nine chapters of the final twenty-seven. In fact, it is found in the central three of that central nine. Indeed, Isaiah 53 is the central chapter of the central three of the central nine of the final twenty-seven chapters of the greatest prophetic book of the Old Testament!

God is concerned about an appropriate setting. We understand this, for we often see a young man come to a time in his life when, at great personal sacrifice, he presents a special gift to a young woman. That gift, a precious stone, is so important that it is placed in an appropriate setting to call attention to its beauty and value. The stone is not simply tossed in the general direction of the young woman who is the object of his affection; rather, it is placed in a setting that is appropriate for it, and usually that setting is a ring made of very precious metal. And if that were not enough, that beautiful ring is put inside a lovely box that is wrapped in pretty paper. Yet, the most important setting for that gift is the loving context in which it is presented.

That is what God has done with this many-faceted jewel of prophetic insight concerning His Son. He put it in the most perfect place so that we simply cannot miss it. We have to believe this prophecy has something very special to say to us.

As we look at the passage, we are amazed to discover, not only how frequently it is *quoted* and how marvelously it is *located*, but also *the form* in which it appears. For thousands of years, prophetic truths concerning Christ were given almost in isolation in the Old Testament—recorded here and there, somewhat as detached details. But here the whole truth is unfolded in a magnificently outlined movement of thought that attracts attention to itself simply by virtue of the form in which it is arranged.

We find three verses of introduction at the end of Isaiah 52. Then the first three verses of chapter 53 tell us of the rejection of the Lord's Servant, beginning at the very start of His earthly career and climaxing with His public rejection. Then, verses 4-6, the heart of the passage and its central three verses, explain the true purpose of His coming: to die, not for His sins, but for the sins of His people. Here is the atonement of Christ, the Servant. Then we back off a bit from this inner, inner sanctum and look in verses 7-9 at the outward circumstances of His crucifixion, suffering, and rejection. These verses describe what actually happened when Jesus Christ died and was buried. Of course, no such picture would be complete without the grand climax of it all, which we find in verses 10-12 in the exaltation and victory of the Servant. These verses describe what really happened as far as God is concerned, focusing on the eternal effects of His work and the basis upon which people can enter into that victory. What a magnificent portrait in prophecy this is of God's unique Savior for mankind!

The Mystery of Jehovah's Servant

We turn now to the introduction in Isaiah 52:13-15, which we call "The Mystery of Jehovah's Servant." Notice the fantastic contrasts here as the text moves from the Servant's ultimate exaltation in verse 13, to the abysmal depths to which He sank at the hands of wicked men in verse 14, and then to what He will do at the end of the age in verse 15. This is a thumbnail sketch of the entire career of the Christ from Bethlehem to the right hand of God the Father.

The Spirit of God is speaking here, and this is His masterpiece. Let us not miss a word.

> *Behold, My Servant shall deal prudently; He shall be exalted and extolled and be very high.* (Isaiah 52:13)

I consider *behold* the special word of the Holy Spirit. By it, He means stop what you are doing, look, and listen because here is God's unique Person for people to behold, relate to, and ponder. Nothing else can compare to seeing the Son of God through the eye of faith and responding to the challenge and commands of God's written Word to concentrate on His Son. The New Testament is full of such commands.

> If then you were raised with Christ, seek those things which are above, where Christ is, sitting at the right hand of God. Set your mind on things above, not on things on the earth. (Colossians 3:1-2).

Set your mind on Him because in Him are hidden "all the treasures of wisdom and knowledge" (Colossians 2:3). "Behold" Christ because there is no Servant like this one.

Israel is called a servant in the book of Isaiah, but Israel frequently failed God and is still failing Him. God has a great purpose for Israel, but as of this moment, it seems to have been a failure.

Cyrus, the Persian king, also is spoken of as God's servant, but he was a pagan and never knew the Lord. Isaiah 45 makes that clear, twice saying to him, "You have not known me" (verses 4-5). Cyrus was a marvelous servant in the universal kingdom of God (not the theocratic kingdom); he was an unwilling, unwitting, and unbelieving instrument, but he was very effective in God's hand, for he released Israel from their Babylonian captivity and sent them back to their promised land to build the second temple and establish the theocracy again. But that pagan servant, called in Isaiah 45:1 the Lord's "anointed," and Israel, God's "servant," were completely inadequate to fit this picture of Jesus Christ as the supreme Servant.

Behold, My Servant shall deal prudently.

This term translated "prudently" means "successfully." It is used in Joshua 1:8 to describe the fantastic success one will have under God if he keeps his eye on the Lord and remembers God's promises in the Scriptures. The Lord Jesus Christ was the most successful servant who ever existed. It is very important to understand this because the tendency in Christendom today (to say nothing of the unregenerate world) is to consider Jesus Christ largely a man of tragedy, suffering, and defeat. Of course, as Isaiah is going to tell us, there is a deep element of tragedy and defeat in the experience of Jesus Christ, but the Spirit of God wants to brace us for that tragedy by anticipating in advance the ultimate victory. It is important to keep the sufferings in perspective so that we can appreciate their purpose.

Paul spoke of his own sufferings in Romans 8, but he kept them in proper perspective.

> For I consider that the sufferings of this present time are not worthy to be compared with the glory which shall be revealed in us. (Romans 8:18)

Let us not underestimate Paul's sufferings in his ministry. They would put our sufferings into the shadow completely. Yet he considered them a light affliction, not to be compared to the glory that is to be revealed.

Many of us like to see in advance how things are going to turn out. Sometimes we see Christian films that terrify us because we do not know how the hero is going to get through the situation. Or in reading a historical novel, following the ups and downs of the hero, we can become very discouraged and tempted to peek at the last chapter to see how it ends.

God wants us to know the last chapter concerning His Son. He wants us to know the final culmination of His Son. He cannot resist telling us that His life is not a tragedy; He is the most successful man who ever lived. If you ask the average person today what he thinks of Jesus of Nazareth, he is likely to remember a great teacher who tried great things but was crushed under the wheel of fate, destroyed by the Roman Empire on a cruel cross two thousand years ago. He tried and was great for a while. His plans were magnificent, but he failed—Jesus Christ superstar. What blasphemy that is, and how sad!

God says He is not a failure. Notice the three descriptions of the measure of his success.

He shall be exalted and extolled and be very high.

Here we see the three steps described in the New Testament of Christ's rise to the highest glory. Note carefully: "He shall be exalted" literally means "He shall rise" and thus speaks of Christ's resurrection from the dead. "Extolled" means "lifted up," describing His ascension to heaven above. His position at the right hand of God the Father is *"very high"*; indeed, it is the highest, most glorious place in the universe. Resurrection, ascension, and exaltation—that is success!

We might also pause and think of another exalted being who said, according to Isaiah 14:14, "I will ascend above the heights of the clouds; I will make myself like the Most High" (NASB). As a result, Lucifer was "cut down to the earth" (Isaiah 14:12). Here Isaiah used the prophetic past tense, as he did throughout these chapters, to portray a future event (see John 12:31) as so certain it can be described as a past event. So Satan, who exalted himself, was and will be abased, and the Lord Jesus, who according to Philippians 2 abased Himself, shall be exalted; and every knee shall bow and every tongue shall confess that He is Lord of all.

Now with that background, we are prepared to take the plunge.

Just as many were astonished at you … (Isaiah 52:14)

Who are the *many* who were astonished? In context, this seems to refer to the nation of Israel. Israel saw, as no other nation has seen, the glorious works of God accomplished through their Messiah, Jesus Christ, in His earthly ministry. They were astonished by His claim to be equal with God, but more than that they were absolutely shocked and offended by it. More than once they picked up stones to stone Him because He claimed equality with God, and they considered Him a mere sinful man like themselves. They knew what He claimed, but they adamantly rejected it and even attempted to destroy Him for making the claim. He made other fantastic claims as well, and they all were backed up by incredible, supernatural sign-miracles, the likes of which Israel had never seen, not even in the days of Moses in Egypt. Hundreds of thousands of Israelites followed Him, saw His miracles, and experienced His power, but now He was humiliated, rejected, and apparently defeated.

The contrast between His marvelous works and claims and His actual condition at the time of crucifixion was probably the primary cause of the stupendous astonishment in the nation of Israel. Look at the details that caused the astonishment.

… so His visage was marred more than any man, and His form more than the sons of men.

These words relate to His physical human appearance as a man. By the time a satanically incensed, hateful nation had vented upon him their total displeasure and turned Him over to the tender mercies of the Roman soldiers, Jesus had been physically reduced to a form that was almost subhuman. He was hardly recognizable as a man.

Note carefully how John describes this in his Gospel in chapter 19. As the scene opens, we see the governor of Judea, Pilate, desperately frustrated. Being a Roman governor, he was under tremendous obligation to dispense justice in his province in the name of the emperor. Pilate did know the difference between justice and injustice, although he rarely practiced justice. He was personally a very wicked person. In fact, he was later deposed and exiled by the Roman emperor in retaliation for his mismanagement of the province of Judea. But he did have a sense of justice that absolutely frustrated him when he was being pressured and manipulated by the Jewish leaders to crucify a man he knew was innocent. In a last desperate attempt to get this thing off his back, he offered the crowd before him a choice: he would release either Jesus or Barabbas. He assumed the Jews obviously would prefer to have Jesus released than a known robber and insurrectionist, but he was mistaken. He underestimated the hatred of the Jews for Jesus Christ.

Earlier, John explained why they hated Jesus, writing,

> And this is the condemnation, that the light has come into the world, and men loved darkness rather than light, because their deeds were evil. For everyone practicing evil hates the light and does not come to the light, lest his deeds should be exposed. (John 3:19-20)

Divine light is the worst possible experience for a depraved, sinful soul. We hate to even think of analogies like this, but when you kick over a rotten log, out come the creatures of darkness, fleeing in terror from the light. In Christ, for the first time in history, the Light had entered the human race visibly, and not merely as an imperfect reflection through some prophet. Here was the incarnate Light, and people with fallen natures, depraved and satanically blinded, could not endure the presence of that Light because it exposed them for what they were and demonstrated their desperate need for repentance and a total turning to God.

Therefore, beyond their own knowledge, they accomplished Satan's purpose when they cried out, "Crucify him!" They were consistent instruments of Satan. They could not stand the Light any more than Satan and his demons can. The demons were terrified when Jesus came, because they knew who He was (cf. Luke 4:34).

The problem is not that people do not know who Jesus is; it is that they *do* know who He is. That is why they hate Him. You cannot hate somebody you do not know. Every person who has entered this world knows who Christ is. John 1:9 says that Christ is the light that lights every person. He created man in His image and likeness, and every human being has indelibly imprinted on his innermost being, the image and identity of Christ the Creator. When Christ the Creator came and, through His word and by the Holy Spirit, proclaimed His identity and authority, there was an intuitive and instantaneous recognition of Him. And there was also an instantaneous hatred of Him. People turned from Him, just as Adam fled from the presence of his Friend—the preincarnate Christ—who revealed Himself to our first parents in the garden.

So the Jewish crowd said they did not want Jesus released. Instead, they wanted the miserable, proven terrorist Barabbas turned loose. With all his experience with horrible people, Pilate surely had never encountered anything like this. In total frustration, he responded by taking Jesus and scourging Him (John 19:1).

Scourging, or flogging, was a horrible thing, a method the Roman soldiers employed to reduce a man practically to ribbons.

> And the soldiers twisted a crown of thorns and put it on His head, and they put on Him a purple robe. Then they said, "Hail, King of the Jews!" And they struck Him with their hands. Pilate then went out again, and said to them, "Behold, I am bringing Him out to you, that you may know that I find no fault in Him." (John 19:2-4)

Pilate brought forth Jesus, this bloody mass of apparent humanity, and displayed Him before the crowd, hoping that in sympathy, they would relent.

> Then Jesus came out, wearing the crown of thorns and the purple robe. And Pilate said to them, "Behold the Man!" (John 19:5)

Then, contrary to Pilate's expectations and hopes, look what they did.

> Therefore, when the chief priests and officers saw Him, they cried out, saying, "Crucify Him, crucify Him!" Pilate said to them, "You take Him and crucify Him, for I find no fault in Him." (John 19:6).

Absolutely despairing of any hope of salvaging his own reputation as a Roman governor, Pilate turned Jesus over to the priests, saying, in essence, "If that is the kind of people you are, go ahead and crucify Him. I'm finished with you people. I can't believe you would do this to this innocent person." In so doing, he crucified his own conscience, activated by his wife's dream and her warning to have nothing to do with that righteous man, Jesus (Matthew 27:19).

Seven hundred years earlier, Isaiah saw the whole scene.

> ***Just as many were astonished at you, so His visage was marred more than any man, and His form more than the sons of men.***

Then that beaten and bloody Person who could not even drag His own cross to Golgotha, pled with His Father to forgive those who had wronged Him, and He pled with John to take care of Mary, His mother. Through His suffering, He showed concern for others and did not complain. One of the most astonished persons of all was a hardened Roman centurion. Seeing Jesus' reactions and attitudes, he said, "Truly this was the Son of God!" (Matthew 27:54). He had never seen anybody like Jesus. There was something genuinely mysterious about this Man, Jesus of Nazareth.

That is how the scene ended almost two thousand years ago. There was awful darkness, symbolized by the sun itself being eclipsed by God, who turned His own face from His Son, as the one who knew no sin was made "sin for us, that we might become the righteousness of God in Him" (2 Corinthians 5:21). Many were astonished, and even God the Father turned away.

Jesus knew why He died. Nevertheless, as a man, He suffered incredibly in His soul as well as in His body, and He cried out, "My God, My God, why have You forsaken Me?" (Matthew 27:46). Both He and the Father knew the reason, and some day when Christ appears at His second coming, the world also will begin to understand why it all happened. Look back to Isaiah 52:15.

So shall He sprinkle many nations. (Isaiah 52:15)

Peter spoke of believers in Christ being sprinkled with His blood (1 Peter 1:2). As the blood the high priest sprinkled upon people and objects brought ceremonial cleansing, so Christ's blood brings cleansing to believers everywhere.

Another possible meaning of this mysterious word *sprinkling* in Isaiah 52:15 is "to startle." Every time the verb is used in the Old Testament, it literally means, "to cause something to leap." And with the exception of this verse, every time the word is used, it is clear what is being caused to "leap" (e.g., "to cause water to leap" [Numbers 19:21] or "to cause blood to leap" [Leviticus 5:9]). However, Isaiah 52:15 does not state what is being caused to leap. I suggest, therefore, that the expression actually means to totally shock the *nations*.

> **Kings shall shut their mouths at Him; for what had not been told them they shall see, and what they had not heard they shall consider.**

At the second coming of Christ, there will be many national leaders ("kings") who have not submitted to Antichrist but have believed "this gospel of the kingdom [which] will be preached [by the 144,000 and others] in all the world as a witness to all the nations" (Matthew 24:14) before the end comes. These leaders of "sheep" nations will be amazed at Christ's glory and grace (Matthew 25:31-40). Isaiah had already been given a glimpse of this event in Isaiah 49:7: "To the One abhorred by the nation, to the Servant of rulers, kings will see and arise, princes will also bow down, because of the LORD who is faithful" (NASB; cf. Isaiah 49:23).

Isaiah's younger contemporary in Jerusalem, Micah, expressed it like this:

> The nations shall see and be ashamed of all their might ...
> They shall crawl from their holes like snakes of the earth.
> They shall be afraid of the Lord our God, and shall fear because of You. (Micah 7:16-17; cf. Psalm 72:8-11)

Their amazement will be vastly greater than that of the queen of Sheba when she stood in the presence of Solomon and said, "I did not believe the words until I came and saw with my own eyes; and indeed the half was not told me." (1 Kings 10:7).

May we be like the apostle Paul, who quoted this amazing verse (Isaiah 52:15) as an encouragement "to preach the gospel, not where Christ was named, lest I should build on another man's foundation" (Romans 15:20-21).

***

Father, speak to us through Your precious book, the Bible, and through this pinnacle of prophetic portraits of the Son of the Living God. Open our hearts to accept Him voluntarily. Dear Lord, may that decision be permanent, because it is God's work in our heart through His Spirit. We pray in Jesus' name. Amen.

❷

THE REJECTION OF CHRIST

Isaiah 53:1-3

Isaiah 53 is the greatest prophecy of the Old Testament and the entire Bible. It is a chapter the Spirit of God emphasizes over and over again by repeated *quotation* in the New Testament. It is a chapter God supremely holds up to view in its Old Testament *location*. And it fascinates the believer by the *form,* or arrangement, the Spirit of God has given to it as an aid to our memory, as we look at the flow of thought from one step to another.

As we have seen, the last three verses of Isaiah 52 serve as an introduction to Isaiah 53. That introduction provides a thumbnail sketch of Christ from Bethlehem to the right hand of the Father, touching on the deep affliction, suffering, and rejection along His way to glory.

Isaiah 53 is the heart of the prophet's message, and it begins with three verses that speak of the rejection of Jehovah's Servant.

> *Who has believed our report? And to whom has the arm of the Lord been revealed? For He shall grow up before Him as a tender plant, and as a root out of dry ground. He has no form or comeliness; and when we see Him, there is no beauty that we should desire Him. He is despised and rejected by men, a Man of sorrows and acquainted with grief. And we hid, as it were, our faces from Him; He was despised, and we did not esteem Him. (Isaiah 53:1-3)*

The prophet Isaiah, by the Holy Spirit, exhibited a fantastic capacity to look thousands of years into the future to a time when Israel, at the second coming of Christ, will finally turn to their Lord and Messiah. In deep humiliation and repentance for their hundreds of years of rejection of their own King, they will look back in contrition and sorrow and utter the very words we read in this chapter of Isaiah. Looking back from the perspective of the Second Coming to the time of Christ's first coming, Israel will ask of themselves in retrospect these two questions:

> **Who has believed our report? And to whom has the arm of the Lord been revealed? (Isaiah 53:1)**

Obviously, the answer to both questions is "very few." What was the report that was rejected? The gospel of the kingdom that John the Baptist, Jesus, and the apostles all proclaimed to the nation of Israel was simply this: God's coming kingdom was at hand because the Messiah who could establish it was present (Matthew 3:1-3; 4:23-25; 10:1-10). And, indeed, the Messiah *would* establish it if the people of Israel would repent of their rebellion against God and accept Jesus of Nazareth as the promised Messiah. It was Israel, not Gentiles, who must repent in order for Christ, the Messiah, to establish the kingdom of heaven on earth. This is why He initially commissioned the Twelve with these words: "Do not go into the way of the Gentiles, and do not enter a city of the Samaritans. But go rather to the lost sheep of the house of Israel. And as you go, preach, saying, 'The kingdom of heaven is at hand'" (Matthew 10:5-7).

Clearly, Israel is the most privileged nation the world has ever known with regard to signs and prophetic revelations from God. It is all inscripturated in a holy book, the Bible. The vast majority of the Bible came from Jewish writers. In fact, the only exceptions are the Gospel of Luke and the book of Acts, both of which were written by the Gentile Luke, the beloved physician. All the other books of the Bible were written by Jews. Yet that very nation, which was specially chosen by God, rejected the message that supremely revealed the nature, power, and glory of God. The nation rejected Jesus as their Messiah, and God's kingdom was not established on earth at that time. That kingdom, for which we pray (cf. Matthew 6:10), will come only when the people of Israel acknowledge Jesus as Messiah and Lord, and that awaits His second coming.

"Who has believed our report?" Not the nation to whom Christ came (John 1:11). Indeed, sadly, very few individuals within the Jewish nation believed or ever have believed what God revealed to them concerning Christ at His first coming. The vast majority of Jewish people today continue to reject the Messiah, in spite of a number of fine mission organizations that are reaching out to them in centers of Jewish populations in this country, in Israel, and around the world. While the number of Jewish believers is growing, as a percentage very few Jewish people acknowledge the Messiah as their Savior.

Through the Holy Spirit, the apostle Paul anticipated that great tragedy in his own experience. He went from synagogue to synagogue in the Mediterranean world and presented the Messiah, explaining from the Old Testament Scriptures—especially Isaiah 53—who Jesus was and how perfectly He fulfilled the Old Testament prophecies. But Paul had to say in Romans 11:5: "Even so then, at this present time there is a remnant according to the election of grace." That's all there was—a tiny remnant. He himself, Saul of Tarsus, was one of them. He was a Jew who had fought Jesus and His followers until the day Jesus met him on the Damascus Road, broke his resistance, and flung him to the ground, blinded and groveling in the dirt, and said to him, "Saul, Saul, why are you persecuting Me? ... It is hard for you to kick against the goads" (Acts 9:4-5).

That is the message the glorified Christ is delivering to every Jew: "Why do you persecute me? It is hard for you to kick against the goads of conscience and the witness that comes to you mostly from Gentile Christians." Now, according to Romans 11, Israel is broken off from God's olive tree, and foreign, or strange, branches have been grafted into that tree. Those branches are Gentiles, not Jews. What a great tragedy in the history of redemption is Israel's rejection of their Messiah.

What does Isaiah mean when he says, "To whom has the arm of the Lord been revealed?" The "arm of the Lord" is a symbol of God's strength and mighty deeds. Throughout the Old Testament, from time to time God revealed Himself in spectacular ways to individuals and to the nation of Israel. Notice how frequently Isaiah mentions the arm (or arms) of the Lord.

> My righteousness is near, My salvation has gone forth, and My arms will judge the peoples; The coastlands will wait upon Me, and on My arm they will trust. (Isaiah 51:5)

In other words, if you see God manifested in one way or another in the universe above, in the earth beneath, or in your own conscience, you had better trust in the arm of God, which God has revealed before the eyes of humanity.

> Awake, awake, put on strength, O arm of the Lord! Awake as in the ancient days, in the generations of old. (Isaiah 51:9)

Here is Isaiah pleading for God to do something in a visible, spectacular way before the eyes of men.

> The Lord has made bare His holy arm in the eyes of all the nations; and all the ends of the earth shall see the salvation of our God. (Isaiah 52:10)

There was never a time in all of human history when God more perfectly and unmistakably revealed Himself in all His power and glory as when His own beloved Son walked the earth. The Son was miraculously conceived, and in the midst of a corrupt and depraved humanity, He lived a miracle life that was perfectly sinless. His was the only uncontaminated human life this world has ever seen. And His prolonged, visible exposure allowed people to observe Him carefully, ask Him questions, and analyze His responses to situations. He "was in all points tempted as we are, yet without sin" (Hebrews 4:15). He was the Lamb of God, absolutely without flaw or blemish, and that was both a rebuke and an astonishment to humanity.

In Jesus Christ, the arm of God was revealed to the human race supremely. Specifically, the revelation of the arm of God in Isaiah 53:1 seems to refer to the miracles Christ and His apostles per-formed as they proclaimed the gospel of the kingdom of heaven (Matthew 10:7-8). Those works so clearly revealed God and His might that they put into the shadow the spectacular things God did at Mount Sinai, when He caused a whole mountain to shake and smoke. They put into shadow the crossings of the Red Sea and the Jordan River and the fire Elijah brought down from heaven on Mount Carmel before the eyes of thousands. Those were spectacular acts, but they did not communicate clearly the character and glory of God as the personal appearance of Jesus did.

Jesus Christ is the supreme revelation of the arm of God before the eyes of mankind. But the question is, "To whom has the arm of the Lord been revealed?" The answer, again, sadly, is very few.

This is the mystery—the mystery of iniquity. God tells us that it is not because the message is unclear or Jesus' claims are debatable. Paul explains that "if our gospel is veiled" (2 Corinthians 4:3)—if people can not hear and believe the message—there is a reason. It is not because they are ignorant; it is because they are lost:

> The god of this world hath blinded the minds of them
> which believe not, lest the light of the glorious gospel of
> Christ, who is the image of God, should shine unto them.
> (2 Corinthians 4:4 KJV)

That is the reason. "We do not wrestle against flesh and blood" or mere human minds when we present Christ. We wrestle against "principalities, against powers, against the rulers of the darkness of this age" (Ephesians 6:12). Satan and demons dominate the unsaved, unregenerate minds of people.

> The natural man does not receive the things of the Spirit
> of God, for they are foolishness to him; nor can he know

21

them, because they are spiritually discerned. (1 Corinthians 2:14)

Jesus Himself revealed in a parable that as the gospel of the kingdom was being proclaimed to the people of Israel, Satan and his emissaries were "snatching away" the seed sown in their hearts, prompting them to reject Jesus as their Messiah and His offer of the kingdom of heaven (Matthew 13:19, 38-39).

Jesus clearly recognized this when He said, "Narrow is the gate and difficult is the way which leads to life, and there are few who find it" (Matthew 7:14).

The answer to the questions in Isaiah 53:1 is very, very few. Verse 2 gives the explanation for why that is.

> **For He shall grow up before Him as a tender plant, and as a root out of dry ground. He has no form or comeliness; and when we see Him, there is no beauty that we should desire Him. (Isaiah 53:2)**

In other words, Jesus came disguised as a mere man. This is what we call in Latin the *incognito* Christ—the unknown and unrecognized One. He did not come flashing down from heaven with a halo over His head and beams coming from His face, smashing all opposition and forcing people to acknowledge His deity. He could have done that, of course, and, in fact, that is what He will do at the Second Coming. But His first coming was *incognito*. He came in such a way that only those who believed His message on the basis of His character, works, and words would have their eyes opened to His identity.

Note carefully the words, "He shall grow up before Him [God]." By the time of Christ's birth, the Jewish people had been looking for the Messiah for hundreds of years. Literature written during the four hundred years between the end of the Old Testament and the birth of Jesus constantly speculated about the coming of the Messiah. However, those writings very conveniently eliminated all the Old Testament prophecies that had to do with His suffering and humiliation (including this one). Instead, they chose to focus only on those verses that tell of His glory and power at the Second Coming, when He will defeat His enemies by His omnipotent word. Passages like Psalm 2 and Daniel 7 were the ones in which they gloried. Therefore, when Jesus came to the earth, not in a flash of glory but through a humble birth in a stable in Bethlehem, and was raised for thirty years in an obscure town called Nazareth, the Jews were deeply offended. When He appeared at the age of thirty and claimed He was the Messiah, they refused to believe.

Matthew 13:54-57 records how Jesus came and taught in His hometown synagogue. The people there were astonished and said:

> "Where did this Man get this wisdom and these mighty works? Is this not the carpenter's son? Is not His mother called Mary? And His brothers James, Joses, Simon, and Judas? And His sisters, are they not all with us? Where then did this Man get all these things?" So they were offended at Him.

In other words, they reasoned that He could not be the Messiah because the Messiah was coming directly from heaven in the clouds of glory with angelic armies, and nations would be destroyed before His irresistible power. This man could not possibly fit that description, because He was born in Palestine, He had grown up among them, and they knew His parents and family.

> But Jesus said to them, "A prophet is not without honor except in his own country and in his own house." Now He did not do many mighty works there because of their unbelief. (Matthew 13:57-58)

The people already had made up their minds. This Person had grown up in their midst and therefore could not be the Messiah. However, Isaiah had said, "He shall grow up before Him as a tender plant, and as a root out of dry ground." The Spirit of God warned the Jewish people seven hundred years in advance that there was a twofold aspect to the coming Messiah, and they missed it deliberately.

I believe the "dry ground" the root came out of refers to the terrible conditions in which Jesus grew up as a boy. Nazareth was a wicked city. In fact, it had such a bad reputation throughout Palestine that Nathanael said, "Can anything good come out of Naza-reth?" (John 1:46). It was a border town between Galilee and Samaria and was looked down upon by the dignified Jews of Jerusalem to the south. They thought the Galileans, and particularly those from Nazareth, were very crude and wicked people. Of course God protected Jesus from the horrible contamination of that city by raising Him in a very poor but godly home. Mary and Joseph loved the Lord and believed the Scriptures. Still, Jesus' own brothers and sisters—later children of Mary and Joseph—did not believe God and rejected Jesus' claims. So, it was indeed a very dry ground for the Son of God to grow up in. We might have expected Jesus to make His appearance in a palace in Rome or at least in Jerusalem, but He was destined to be a despised person. This is what Matthew was referring to when he spoke of Jesus and His parents moving to Nazareth following their return from their flight into Egypt.

> And he came and dwelt in a city called Nazareth, that it might be fulfilled which was spoken by the prophets, "He shall be called a Nazarene." (Matthew 2:23)

It was not only Jesus' poverty-stricken family and despised hometown that were so unpalatable to the Jews; His very appearance also was an unforgivable offence to them.

He has no form or comeliness; and when we see Him, there is no beauty that we should desire Him.

This does not mean Jesus was ugly. Artists in the Middle Ages picked up this statement and deliberately painted pictures of Jesus that they thought looked frightening and repulsive. He was constantly portrayed in paintings from the fifth to the ninth centuries as one who frowned and scowled at people. That was totally erroneous. Jesus was not repulsive or frightening in His appearance. Little children flocked to Him, and the common people heard Him gladly. The Hebrew words used here suggest that the outward paraphernalia of a king, the trappings of royalty, are primarily in view. That is what the Jewish people were looking for. They were accustomed to seeing Roman senators parading through their cities with men running before their chariots and soldiers blowing bugles and clearing the streets. The important Roman dignitaries would come robed appropriately in spectacular garments. Surely, the Jewish people thought their Messiah would be just as impressive—and more so!

Almost certainly Jesus did not set foot in a chariot in His entire thirty-three years on planet Earth. Not one soldier prepared the way for him by blowing trumpets. As a matter of fact, if you saw Jesus of Nazareth coming to the temple in Jerusalem on one of the special festival days during His ministry, you would have seen a humble, common-looking man in the simple garb of a Galilean peasant, being followed by a motley crew of fishermen and one ex-tax collector. Most of the Jews could never imagine that such a person could be their Messiah, the Son of God. He lacked the form, the dignity, the spectacular appearance they expected and desired. He did not even have a place to lay His head; He had no head-quarters and no army. And so they were shocked and offended at His claim to be the Messiah and God in the flesh.

The Jewish people had been warned ahead of time in Isaiah 53:2, but they deliberately rejected their Messiah. They were embarrassed to have to admit to themselves and to the Gentiles around them that their king would look like Jesus.

The people of Israel had faced the same problem a thousand years before Jesus came. When people came to Jerusalem to see their king, they had to say He was invisible. No one could see their King, Jehovah, because He was in heaven. They became so embarrassed by the absence of a visible king that they finally came to Samuel the prophet and demanded a king "like all the nations" (1 Samuel 8:5). They wanted a visible, spectacular king with an army and a throne.

Both Samuel and God were heartbroken, but God gave the people a king after their own hearts, and said in effect, "He will do what you want your king to do for you. When you cry out in agony, do not come back to Me, because you are getting what you want." Their king's name was Saul, and he was a great tragedy for the nation of Israel.

Israel has never learned that their God, although invisible, is infinite in power and glory and can deliver them from all their enemies. So, when they saw Jesus, who by all outward appearance was unimpressive and certainly not the kind of king they desired, they refused to accept Him as king. They did not have the mind of our Lord Jesus Christ,

> who, being in the form of God, did not consider it robbery to be equal with God, but made Himself of no reputation, taking the form of a bondservant, and coming in the likeness of men. And being found in appearance as a man, He humbled Himself and became obedient to the point of death, even the death of the cross. (Philippians 2:6-8)

This is the mind Paul said we are to have. Forget the outward show. God will take care of our reputation, influence, and impact on people's lives. The outward show is never God's way but is an abomination to Him.

There was one occasion when Jesus gave to human beings a glimpse of how glorious He is. That was up on top of a mountain, and only three people saw it—the inner three, of the inner twelve, of the seventy, of the five hundred who were His disciples. Only Peter, James, and John had the privilege of seeing Jesus there, as He was "transfigured before them" (Matthew 17:2) and met with Moses and Elijah, and even they misunderstood the meaning of this event. Peter wanted to build three tabernacles there and stay on the mountaintop. God had to tell the disciples to look at Jesus only, in all His splendor and glory.

God is not interested in overpowering people with outward appearances. That is why the apostle Paul, who had the mind of the Spirit and was the true representative of the mind of Christ for the church, said something very interesting in 2 Corinthians 5:16. This verse sounds very strange, but Paul, speaking of the love of Christ that constrained him and of the Christ who died that we might live not for ourselves but for Him, said this:

> Therefore, from now on, we regard no one according to the flesh. Even though we have known Christ according to the flesh, yet now we know Him thus no longer.

In other words, Paul was sick and tired of outward appearances, titles, robes, crowns, thrones, palaces, and chariots. He was looking at the inner man.

People today desperately want to have a picture of Jesus Christ Himself. They want to know what He looked like. They want to have a painting or a shroud with His image. The Bible does not give one word, from Genesis to Revelation, as to what Christ, the Son of God, looked like physically. Christ wants us to see Him through the eye of faith as the Bible describes His glory and dignity and purpose in coming as God's Son and our Savior. And even if we had seen Him in the flesh, God's Word says that would not help us spiritually. It does not matter how many pictures of Jesus we have hanging on our walls; we are dead in trespasses and sins unless we see His true dignity and identity as revealed by the Holy Spirit through the Bible. I am not saying we need to throw out our pictures; I am just saying that not one of them is an accurate representation of what Jesus looked like. Nobody knows what He looked like outwardly, and it does not make any difference.

We are saved by faith, not by sight. Thousands saw Jesus and shouted, "Crucify Him!" Millions have never seen Him, yet they have entrusted their eternal destiny to Him. Jesus said, "Blessed are those who have not seen and yet have believed." (John 20:29).

> ***He is despised and rejected by men, a Man of sorrows and acquainted with grief. And we hid, as it were, our faces from Him; He was despised, and we did not esteem Him.*** **(Isaiah 53:3)**

Oh, what sledgehammer blows this verse deals to man's ideals of what a savior should be like. You will not see in this passage any Hollywood image of a man of distinction; you will not see the American ideal of what the successful man should look like and what he should wear and where he should live. Not one of those ideals was met by the Son of God at His first coming. And that is why He was "despised and rejected of men."

Nibzeh (the simple passive form of the verb *bazah*) is a powerful word in Hebrew that is translated "despised" here. There is hardly a word in English that is appropriate and adequate to describe the intense hatred Israel heaped upon Jesus of Nazareth.

The word for men (*ishim*), in the phrase "rejected by men," means "men of distinction." There are various Hebrew words for man. *Adam* refers to man from the ground. *Enosh* is a man of weakness. But *ish* denotes a man of dignity. Jesus was despised by men of dignity. The New Testament tells us who those men of dignity (*ishim*) were who despised and rejected the Lord. John 7 describes a confrontation between the rulers of Israel (the men of distinction) and a believer in Jesus named Nicodemus. The leaders of Israel had sent officers to capture Jesus and bring Him back alive to destroy Him (John 7:32). At the end of the day, they came back empty-handed. When asked why, the officers said, "No man ever spoke like this Man!" (John 7:46).

> Then the Pharisees answered them, "Are you also deceived? Have any of the rulers or the Pharisees believed in Him? But this crowd that does not know the law is accursed." (John 7:47-49)

In other words, they said, "You are cursed, ignorant people to believe in Jesus. Have any of the intelligentsia taken His claims seriously?"

But then Nicodemus—the most brilliant and authoritative of all the Old Testament scholars, a man who had previously come to Jesus by night and met the Savior (John 3)—courageously stood up.

> Nicodemus (he who came to Jesus by night, being one of them) said to them, "Does our law judge a man before it hears him and knows what he is doing?" They answered and said to him, "Are you also from Galilee? Search and look, for no prophet has arisen out of Galilee." And everyone went to his own house. (John 7:50-53)

They were wrong. The prophet Jonah had come from Galilee, as their Scriptures taught (2 Kings 14:25); and more important, Isaiah said that out of Galilee the Light (in the person of the Messiah) would come (Isaiah 9:1-2). They missed that prophecy. Now, with the single exception of Nicodemus, all the leaders, intelligentsia, and powerful people despised and rejected the Lord Jesus. The common people and the children heard Him gladly. Sadly, times have not changed. Paul told the Corinthians:

> For you see your calling, brethren, that not many wise according to the flesh, not many mighty, not many noble, are called. But God has chosen the foolish things of the world to put to shame the wise, and God has chosen the weak things of the world to put to shame the things which are mighty; and the base things of the world and the things which are despised God has chosen, and the things which are not, to bring to nothing the things that are, that no flesh should glory in His presence. (1 Corinthians 1:26-29)

How many of the great leaders of the world really believe in Jesus? How many of the leaders of the ecumenical church movement today really believe in Jesus Christ and His Word? Times have not changed: the religious leaders were ultimately responsible for putting Jesus on the cross. He was despised and rejected by men of authority.

... a man of sorrows and acquainted with grief

Throughout the brief public ministry of the Lord Jesus, there was a constant combination of two things: sorrow and grief. Jesus had the unique capacity to see the whole life story of every human being with whom the Father brought Him into personal contact.

Wearied from His journey, Jesus sat down at a well in Samaria. When a woman came to the well, Jesus asked her for water, seeking to engage her in conversation. In deep love for this woman, and in order to win her to the living God, He said to her, "Call your husband." She said, "I have no husband." He said, "You have well said, 'I have no husband,' for you have had five husbands, and the one whom you now have is not your husband; in that you spoke truly" (John 4:16-18). She was terrified because Jesus knew all about her.

Elsewhere Jesus said, "As My Father taught Me, I speak these things" (John 8:28). That means that all the sordid background and deep depravity of every human being He ministered to was an open book before Him. Certainly, that would not produce joy but sorrow. If you knew the background and eternal destiny of every unsaved person you met, you would be filled with sorrow as well. Yet at the same time, Jesus was a man of deep joy. The apostle Paul, who on the one hand could say he was constantly burdened with heaviness because of his people Israel (Romans 9:1-5), could also say, "Rejoice in the Lord always. Again I will say, rejoice!" (Philippians 4:4).

That horizontal look into the true spiritual condition of people and their eternal destiny in the hands of the living God creates intense sorrow. Yet, there is deep joy in the vertical view, seeing what God is doing and what He will accomplish in His day and time. Thus, Jesus could say in the upper room, "These things I have spoken to you, that My joy may remain in you, and that your joy may be full" (John 15:11). He experienced both infinite joy and infinite sorrow.

The word translated "grief" literally means "sicknesses" or "diseases." Every human being has a fallen nature and the visible results of that fallenness: namely, a diseased body. Every human being today exists as a visible end product of the downward processes that were initiated by the fall of man at the dawn of history. The shortness of our life span compared to that of Adam, our genetic pollution evidenced by the amazing percentage of defective births that are due to genetic inheritance, and the downward drag of human depravity in terms of international social, economic, educational, and political chaos are its results. Our body is, in the biblical sense, diseased because of sin. Even the apostle Paul had a diseased body; and he cried out to God three times for healing, but God said no (2 Corinthians 12:7-9). In Romans 8:22-23 Paul also said,

> For we know that the whole creation groans and labors with birth pangs together until now. Not only that, but we also who have the firstfruits of the Spirit, even we ourselves groan within ourselves, eagerly waiting for the adoption, the redemption of our body.

Not until resurrection day will we discover how physically diseased and sickly our present system is.

If you are a believer, there is an incredible contrast between what you are now and what you will be when God gets through with you on resurrection day. When you trusted Christ as your Savior, you became a new creation in reference to Jesus and entered into a new relationship. You became a member of God's mystical body in Christ, and the Holy Spirit moved into your body as His temple. However, you will have to wait until resurrection or rapture to get your new body. This is phase two of the redemptive work of Jesus upon the cross for you and me. Your new body will not be like your present one. It will not be subject to sin and the ravages of disease and sickness that sin brings forth. This man of sorrows and grief will take care of your sorrows and diseases forever, and you will have joy in His presence forevermore.

And we hid, as it were, our faces from Him; He was despised, and we did not esteem Him.

This simply summarizes the whole history of the human race from Adam to this moment: full-time hiding from Him. But if a person is open to God, then God's Word will pour into that person's mind and soul and bring an immediate response of faith, obedience, and love.

> "'You shall love the Lord your God with all your heart, with all your soul, with all your strength, and with all your mind,' and 'your neighbor as yourself.'" (Luke 10:27)

Anyone who cannot attest to such love for God and others is hiding his or her face from Him, resisting Him, turning from Him, and suppressing the truth. And this is the course taken by all unregenerate humanity.

Adam hid behind trees, but people have discovered that trees are inadequate hiding places from God. Now, they hide behind their supposed reputations, good works in the community, and even church membership or baptism. God will penetrate all of those outward things and come to the heart of the matter.

> For the word of God is living and powerful, and sharper than any two-edged sword, piercing even to the division of soul and spirit, and of joints and marrow, and is a discerner of the thoughts and intents of the heart. And there is no creature hidden from His sight, but all things are naked and open to the eyes of Him to whom we must give account. (Hebrews 4:12-13)

There is no use hiding from God; He sees us and knows us. There is only one thing to do—surrender unconditionally on His terms.

Every human being who has trusted Jesus has two parts in his or her life: BC and AD, before Christ and after. That is what this passage means when it says, "We did not esteem him." Before Christ came into our lives, we esteemed Him not. "Esteemed" means to reckon Him into every phase of our thinking and living. When we awake in the morning, we thank Him for sparing us during the night and ask for His guidance through the day. And at the end of our day, we say, "Thank You for watching over me; forgive me for my disobedience, neglect, and sin." We need to acknowledge Him in all things and walk in the light as He is in the light. This is esteeming Him. Before Christ entered our lives, we did not reckon

Him as the center of everything. But, thank God, by His grace, He loved us first; and to some extent, in the light of that love, we love Him.

Do we esteem Him? Do we reckon Him number one in our lives? Or do we despise Him and hide our faces from Him? God will not let us do that forever. He will find us and meet us. But if it is at the Great White Throne (Revelation 20:11), it will be too late. Come to Him now. Accept Him, and love and obey Him.

***

Father, we thank You for Your precious book, the Bible, and we thank You for the blessed Holy Spirit who searches our souls and examines our hearts with infinite tenderness and incomparable light. Please open our hearts for divine surgery that we might see Christ in all of His beauty and glory as Your own Son. Speak to us, we pray, in Jesus' name. Amen.

3

THE DEATH OF CHRIST

Isaiah 53:4-6

Isaiah 53 beautifully divides itself into four three-verse sections, with another three verses in the preceding chapter (Isaiah 52:13-15) forming an introduction to the prophecy. That introduction outlines the entire story of the life and career of Jesus Christ the Lord. Chapter 53 then starts the story all over again with Jesus' humble beginnings and growth in the most unexpected place—Nazareth—and climaxes in verse 12 with His exaltation to heaven. In these twelve verses of Isaiah 53, we follow, step by step, the response of Israel to Jesus, from His total rejection by the nation in verses 1-3, through His atoning death upon the cross in verses 4-6 and the circumstances of His death in verses 7-9, to the culmination, goal, and fulfillment of it all in verses 10-12.

So in verses 4, 5, and 6 of Isaiah 53, we come to the very heart of the prophecy in terms of both its central location and its meaning and purpose; namely, the atoning work of Jesus Christ. This is why Jesus came into the world: to be the Substitute for sinners and to bear their guilt before a holy God.

Earlier Old Testament prophecies concerning Christ are found in Genesis 3:15, Genesis 12 and 49, and in Balaam's prophecy in Numbers 24. Other messianic prophecies are given in Deuteronomy 18, 1 Samuel 2, 2 Samuel 7, Psalms 2, 72, and 110, as well as in the earlier prophecies of the book of Isaiah in chapters 4, 7, 9, and 11, and then the more concentrated and detailed prophetic preview in chapters 40, 42, 49, and 50. These earlier prophecies develop two main lines of thought concerning the Messiah: (1) He is both God and man in one Person, and (2) He must suffer as well as reign as King.

But now, in Isaiah 53, for the first time, we find a prophecy that clearly tells us *why* He will suffer—for our sins, not His own. That is the supreme significance of Isaiah 53. It reveals the substitutionary death of Christ, not merely His death as the representative of all sinful men before a holy God. That is why this three-verse section of the chapter is the inner, inner sanctum of the Holy of Holies of the temple of God's revelation in Scripture concerning the real purpose of His Son.

Isaiah 53 gives us more insight and details on *why* Christ died than even the four Gospels in the New Testament. Thus, it seems the Holy Spirit wants us to look at this chapter to find the real reason for Christ's death and presupposes that we have this foundation already in our hearts and minds when we come to the Gospels. The Gospels then fill in more details on how exactly these events happened, under what circumstances, and over what periods of time.

So the New Testament presupposes a mastery of the Old Testament. I suspect that is why most of us do not know too much about our Bible. We know only the capstone and have lost touch with the thousands of truths God revealed in the Old Testament to prepare the way for a deeper understanding and appreciation of the last twenty-seven books of the Bible we call the New Testament. And here is the heart of it all. Listen carefully to the words.

> *Surely He has borne our griefs and carried our sorrows; yet we esteemed Him stricken, smitten by God, and afflicted. But He was wounded for our transgressions, He was bruised for our iniquities; the chastisement for our peace was upon Him, and by His stripes we are healed. All we like sheep have gone astray; we have turned, every one, to his own way; and the Lord has laid on Him the iniquity of us all. (Isaiah 53:4-6)*

Every word is precisely chosen by the Holy Spirit of God to hammer home the heart of the message—the good news of a Substitute for human sinners.

As the passage begins in verse 4, we see the contrast between what really happened upon the cross as God understood it and planned it and what we thought was going on at the cross. The *we* refers to the Jews and Romans, who stood by and watched; but it also encompasses all lost sinners in rebellion against God and His

ways, who are represented by those Jews and Romans.

In verse 3, we saw that people hid their faces from the Lord's Servant and despised Him and esteemed Him not. They did not appreciate Him or recognize Him for what He was; they did not love Him, surrender to Him, or serve Him. In fact, they did just the opposite: they hated Him. But while they were hating and misunderstanding Him, He was bearing our griefs and carrying our sorrows.

We also recall from verse 3 that Jesus was acquainted with grief and that the word translated "grief" really means "diseases." Disease or sickness is the physical effect of a sinful heart. We must be careful here, however. We cannot declare in individual cases that someone is sick because he or she is more wicked than somebody else. Rather, what is in view here is human frailty in general. The fact that we live such short lives and experience pain and suffering is due to the possession of a sin nature. In fact, when we are glorified, there will be no more sin and, as a result, no more suffering, tears, or pain.

There is a clear connection between sin and disease in the Bible. However, Jesus bore our griefs, or diseases (Isaiah 53:4). This verse is quoted and explained in the New Testament in Matthew 8. We read in verse 16 that many brought demon-possessed people to Jesus, and He cast out the evil spirits with His word and healed all who were sick. Matthew 8:17 then explains why Jesus did this:

... that it might be fulfilled which was spoken by Isaiah the prophet, saying: "He Himself took our infirmities and bore our sicknesses."

Matthew says that the physical healings Jesus performed in His earthly ministry were a fulfillment of Isaiah 53:3-4. That seems strange because if that is the fulfillment of it, then surely not many people have benefited from this work of our Lord Jesus. Jesus is not healing people today as He did then. But when Isaiah 53 says that He bore our griefs, it is speaking of all those who have ever trusted in God, and who therefore enter into a substitutionary work called *bearing*. At the cross He secured for us the healing we will experience at the time of our resurrection or rapture, when we receive new, incorruptible, disease-free bodies (1 Corinthians 15:50-53). The healings in Matthew 8:16-17 thus constitute a partial fulfillment of Isaiah 53:3-4 that anticipated Christ's work at Calvary and the eternal state when there will be no sin or sickness.

The Bible itself tells us that Jesus did not come to this planet two thousand years ago merely to heal human bodies and make people feel better. We know from the New Testament that our faith in God does not determine how physically well we are or how free of diseases and healthy we are. That is a total distortion today that often parades under the name of "faith healing." We must understand that most of the people Jesus healed did not have faith. Jesus healed a group of ten lepers at one time, but only one of them believed and thanked Him (Luke 17:11-19). Nine were unbelievers, yet they were healed anyway. And surely when Jesus said to Lazarus in the tomb, "Come forth," the dead Lazarus had no capacity for faith; but he came out of the tomb anyway (John 11:43-44)!

So, in the New Testament, instantaneous, complete physical healing had nothing to do with the recipient's degree of faith. In some cases, Jesus used healing as a test of faith or at least an encouragement to faith, but it had no necessary connection to faith at all.

Matthew 9:1-6 demonstrates this truth. The scene opens with a description of a desperately sick man, sick of the palsy and totally paralyzed. Four of his friends carried him to Jesus, hoping the Lord would heal him. Jesus looked at the man and said,

> "Son, be of good cheer; your sins are forgiven you." And at once some of the scribes said within themselves, "This Man blasphemes!" But Jesus, knowing their thoughts, said, "Why do you think evil in your hearts? For which is easier, to say, 'Your sins are forgiven you,' or to say, 'Arise and walk'?" (Matthew 9:2-5).

The answer to Jesus' question was obvious. It is much easier to say to a person, "Your sins are forgiven" than it is to say to a lame person, "Arise and walk." You can tell a man his sins are forgiven, but neither he nor anyone else can be sure that it has happened. But when you say to a paralyzed person, "Arise and walk," you had better be sure that person is in fact going to rise up and walk, or you are going to be exposed instantly as a fake.

There are many so-called religious leaders in the world today who love to present themselves as sin-forgivers. They go here and there, laying their hands on people, or pronouncing various formulas, or sprinkling holy water and saying, "Your sins are forgiven"; and absolutely nothing happens. Only God can forgive sin, and God forgives sin only under special circumstances and conditions that He announces in the Bible, namely, faith in the substitutionary work of Jesus His Son. No mere man can forgive anyone's sins.

The enemies of Jesus were correct in that they understood that nobody but God can forgive sin (cf. Mark 2:7). They were wrong, however, in charging Jesus with blasphemy. Their mistake was that they did not realize that it was God the Son who was there forgiving the man his sin. They did not understand who Jesus was and therefore did not believe the man's sins were forgiven. In order to prove that the man was forgiven, Jesus asked him to rise and walk. The miraculous healing demonstrated the power and authority behind Jesus' words of forgiveness. The reason he healed the man was not simply to help the man or to prove that there is a God in heaven. Rather, the healing was designed to attract attention to Himself as the Messiah who had unique power to forgive sin on earth.

> "But that you may know that the Son of Man has power on earth to forgive sins"—then He said to the paralytic, "Arise, take up your bed, and go to your house." (Matthew 9:6)

Jesus is the only man who has ever lived who can forgive sins.

> And he arose and departed to his house. Now when the multitudes saw it, they marveled and glorified God, who had given such power to men. (Matthew 9:7-8)

Let us get the message clearly. As Jesus traveled around Palestine, He healed thousands of people. In fact, when we add up all the statements in the four Gospels that Jesus healed everyone who came to him, it is entirely possible that for that brief period of Palestinian history, every sick, lame, or leprous person in Palestine was healed. Most of them remained unbelievers, but Jesus healed them all. Jesus' powerful healing work, however, was not meant to prove that God will always do the extraordinary in order to relieve the sick and disabled. There are millions of ill and suffering people all over the world today, and God is not healing them. Neither were Jesus' miraculous healings designed to prove that there is a God in heaven who can heal people. The Jewish people knew that, and the Pharisees certainly knew that. There was only one purpose in Jesus' healings: to prove that Jesus of Nazareth was the Messiah of Israel and that He could do that which is greater than healing—forgive sins. Healing bodies was a visual aid and a means to attract attention to the Messiah so that people would believe His message and the explanation of who He was and why He was there.

The Lord Jesus had to do that only once and only for Israel. He is not doing that anymore. There are no more sign-miracles taking place in the world today, deliberately designed by God to attract attention to a man who can forgive sins. That is over; it was accomplished in the life and ministry of Jesus, once for all.

Isaiah 35:5-6 says that when this Messiah comes back again and establishes His kingdom, every person who enters the kingdom will be physically healed. The lame will leap like the hart, and the blind will see. The Bible describes the physical afflictions God's people will endure at the hand of the Antichrist during the future Tribulation. If not for God's shortening those days to three and a half years, no flesh would survive (Matthew 24:22). By the time Jesus comes back, the 144,000 believers and other witnesses who have not yet been martyred will stagger into the kingdom age blind, crippled, and emaciated. Jesus describes this in Matthew 25:31-40. Then Jesus will heal them all, just as He did at His first coming, as a sign of His messianic authority as King of Kings and Lord of Lords.

Do not ever pay any attention to a self-appointed faith healer. Nobody today can do the miracles Jesus did. He could take a man's severed ear and put it right back on his head (Luke 22:50-51). Would you like a valid test for a modern-day "faith healer"? Take a severed portion of your body such as a finger or toe, and rush it to the nearest faith healer, and ask him to put it back on. You will expose him. Ask him to do what Jesus did at the tomb of Lazarus: raise a loved one from the dead after the body has been decomposing for more than half a week. You will quickly learn this one is not a truly anointed representative of the living God in terms of sign-miracles of bodily healing. There is none of that going on today, because the foundation of the church has been laid and the messianic credentials of Jesus have been established before Israel through the apostles and the church.

The next healing event will not be at the beginning of the Millennium, when those who enter the kingdom age alive are healed, but rather seven years earlier at the resurrection and rapture of every Christian when Jesus comes for His church. The first mass healing event we will see in God's program will not be found in some tent meeting but in every grave that contains the body of a person who loved and knew Jesus Christ. "The dead in Christ shall rise first. Then we who are alive and remain shall be caught up together with them in the clouds to meet the Lord in the air. And thus we shall always be with the Lord" (1 Thessalonians 4:17-18). We will have glorified bodies and be totally healed. He has borne our disease; He paid the price, and our bodies will reflect the full down payment of Jesus' blood according to Isaiah 53:4. If He can do that to our body, He surely can take care of our soul as well.

> ***Surely He has borne our griefs and carried our sorrows. (Isaiah 53:4)***

He is the sorrow-bearer—the expert. We cannot do it ourselves. Jesus said:

> "Come to Me, all you who labor and are heavy laden, and I will give you rest. Take My yoke upon you and learn from Me, for I am gentle and lowly in heart, and you will find rest for your souls." (Matthew 11:28-29)

Do not ever try to bear your own sorrows. Do not try to resurrect the dead body of a loved one. Christ is the expert God has appointed to take care of your sorrows as well as your resurrection. He alone will handle it—not modern science but Jesus Christ. Believe it; it is written.

When Christ died upon the cross, we (i.e., Israel) thought of Him as stricken.

> ***Yet we esteemed Him stricken, smitten by God, and afflicted.***

That word "stricken" translates a Hebrew word that is often used of leprosy. King Uzziah, who had reigned for forty years in Judah with great prosperity and brilliance, became so proud that he could not stand the thought of being a mere king. A satanic thought was cultivated in his heart, and he marched into the Holy Place, usurping the privilege of offering incense on the golden altar of incense before God as a priest-king. The pagan nations had priest-kings but not Israel. One could be a king if he was from the tribe of Judah and the family of David; or one could be a priest if he was from the tribe of Levi and the family of Aaron. But no one could be a priest-king. God reserves that privilege for Jesus only. However, Uzziah thought it was not enough to be a king; he wanted to be a priest also. He walked into the temple and defied those priests who withstood him. Then, suddenly, God struck him with leprosy, and he became as white as snow. The priests did not have to push him out of the temple; he fled in terror from the presence of the God who had "struck" him (2 Chronicles 26:20). The chronicler used the same Hebrew verb that is translated "stricken" in Isaiah 53:4.

Anyone who was hanged upon a tree in Israel was cursed of God (Deuteronomy 21:23). That was the mark of a cursed man, one "stricken" by God. Isaiah foresaw the One who had claimed to be God hanging on a cross on a little hill near Jerusalem. Crucifixion was the most horrible, despicable death imaginable in the ancient world. The Jews wondered why, if He was the Son of God as He claimed, He did not come down off the cross. We know why. One artist had the answer straight when he painted a picture of Jesus hanging upon the cross but deliberately left out the nails from His hands and feet. Some thought he forgot this detail, but he explained that nails did not hold Jesus there; love held Him there. That was why He was on the cross.

Jesus could have pulled those nails out of the cross and come down and killed His enemies. Jesus said that if He needed help, He could call for twelve legions of angels (Matthew 26:53). A legion in the Roman army consisted of six thousand soldiers. So, seventy-two thousand angels were at the ready and could have made mincemeat of that Roman detachment at the cross. All Jesus had to do was ask, and that would have been the end of all opposition, and His kingdom would have started right there.

When a small army armed with staves and clubs came to arrest Him in the Garden of Gethsemane, Jesus, the Son of God, asked whom they were seeking. When they said, "Jesus of Nazareth," He answered, "I am," and they all fell backward, crushed by an unseen hand (John 18:5-6). One of the most amazing things in the Bible is that they all got up again and moved toward Jesus! If they had gotten the message, they would have fled in utter terror. This awesome display of Jesus' power was just a little sample of what will happen at the Second Coming.

Jesus' enemies looked at Him and said, "Look, He cannot come down from the cross, He is helpless and defeated. He is 'stricken, smitten by God.'" They committed the fallacy of Job's friends, who told Job day after day that he was suffering in exact proportion to his sin. The unbelieving Jews looked at Jesus and the horrible suffering He had endured at the hands of the Romans through the scourging, the crown of thorns, and the cross and concluded that

His suffering was final proof that He was wicked. They could not possibly have been more wrong.

Let us not make the same mistake in judging others. Let us not think those who are disabled or diseased must deserve their plight because of their wickedness. And let us not think our own health and strength is a proof of virtue and spiritual superiority. Some of God's choicest saints have been the greatest sufferers of all. The apostle Paul was one of them. In fact, in essence, he said to Timothy, "Sorry about your frequent infirmities and stomach problems. I have no faith healer to recommend, and no provision to guarantee instantaneous healing through miracle or faith. Just switch your diet and try something else to drink" (see 1 Timothy 5:23).

Jesus was sinless, and He was not defeated.

> **But He was wounded for our transgressions, He was bruised for our iniquities; the chastisement for our peace was upon Him, and by His stripes we are healed. (Isaiah 53:5)**

This is why Jesus was suffering. It was not for His own sins but for your sins and mine and for the sins of every human being who has ever lived (cf. 1 John 2:2). Those words are powerful in the Hebrew. They are greatly modified in English, almost to the point that the message is lost. Indeed, we must confess that the depth, mystery, and marvel of the nuances of meaning that are locked into the original Hebrew words the Spirit of God inspired, as well as the original Greek words of the New Testament, have never been fully fathomed. Verse 5 is just a little sampler.

"He was wounded for our transgressions" literally means He was pierced through with a fatal blow. The Hebrew verb *chalal* is a violent word. Look back at Isaiah 51:9 to see how it is used.

> Awake, awake, put on strength, O arm of the Lord! Awake
> as in the ancient days, in the generations of old. Are You
> not the arm that cut Rahab apart, and wounded the ser-
> pent?

"Wounded" here represents the same Hebrew verb used in Isaiah 53:5, which means "to destroy by a fatal blow." The dragon is Satan. God did not just wound Satan at the cross; He struck a fatal blow. In the process, Jesus too was struck, not by Satan but by God the Father.

Is it not interesting that in Isaiah's day nobody was executed in Israel by being pierced through? One could be stoned to death, beheaded, or hanged, but no one was crucified. That was a horrible and agonizing death that the tender mercies of the Romans adopted and perfected hundreds of years later. However, the Spirit of God knew the method by which Jesus would die, and three hundred years before Isaiah, the first hint came in Psalm 22:16: "They pierced My hands and My feet." And two hundred years after Isaiah, Zechariah wrote, "They will look on Me whom they have pierced" (Zechariah 12:10). Interestingly, those are three different Hebrew verbs for "pierced," just so we will not miss the message.

Revelation 1:7 says of Christ, "Every eye will see Him, even they who pierced him." Through all eternity, God had planned that His Son would die an agonizing death through a piercing.

He was bruised for our iniquities.

Here again is a modified, softened translation of the original Hebrew verb. Jesus was not just wounded or bruised; He was crushed! The Hebrew verb translated "bruised" is *daka,* from which comes the word for dust. If you take a lump of dirt and smash and pulverize it, you get dust. As the Son of God, the God-man, hung upon the cross, God the Father poured upon Him all the sins of every person who has ever lived. Jesus was totally crushed under the infinite weight of human sin.

When you use a magnifying glass to focus the rays of the sun on one spot, an intense heat is produced. At the cross, it was as if God put over the head of Jesus a magnifying glass to concentrate His wrath for every human being upon one head. One man could not endure the eternal hell that all wicked humanity deserved, but Jesus was not a mere man; He was the God-man, with infinite capacity to suffer eternal hell in minutes because of His eternal, divine nature, character, and attributes and His human nature and body.

The mystery of the cross is that God, being spirit, cannot die because death means separation of body from spirit. So the only way human beings could have their sins atoned for was for a substitute to die in their place. God designed a special, unique plan whereby the second person of the Godhead could become a human being and have a body, so that He could have His body separated from His spirit by death and therefore be the substitute for human sin. No mere human could have designed such a scheme as this. It is a perfect provision for human need.

> ***The chastisement for our peace was upon Him, and by His stripes we are healed.***

Every healing we will ever need was accomplished because Christ bore the chastisement that alone could bring peace between us and our God.

John 3:16 is probably the most familiar verse in the New Testament—and rightly so. It reads,

> For God so loved the world that He gave His only begotten Son, that whoever believes in Him should not perish but have everlasting life.

Now listen to the Old Testament version of John 3:16.

> ***All we like sheep have gone astray; we have turned, every one, to his own way; and the Lord has laid on Him the iniquity of us all.*** (Isaiah 53:6)

Notice how Isaiah 53:6 begins with universal need and ends with universal provision. Nobody who is unaware of his or her need for a Savior wants a Savior. Nobody is going to go to a doctor to have a leg amputated if that person does not recognize the desperate need for that to happen. I do not want my leg amputated unless a group of surgeons can convince me that if I do not have my leg removed, I am going to die. If you are not convinced by God through His prophets that you have an infinite problem—namely sin against a holy God—you are never going to come to Jesus Christ and unconditionally surrender to Him as your Savior. You are not going to place any value on His blood as God's remedy for a problem you do not recognize.

Like sheep, we have all gone astray. The Hebrew word is literally "flock," which pictures the whole human race as a unit. A flock of sheep will follow the lead sheep no matter where it goes—even over a cliff! They will blindly follow the leader, even to death. This is God's explanation of human history. In Adam we all sinned. Adam deliberately and openly defied his God, and every one of us has followed his lead ever since.

> Wherefore, as by one man sin entered into the world, and
> death by sin; and so death passed upon all men, for that
> all have sinned. (Romans 5:12 KJV)

You might question how one man sinning at the dawn of history could be the cause of our sin nature, sorrow, and death. The answer is in this verse: "We have turned, every one, to his own way." Universal sin is explained by individual sin. In other words, every one of us, according to the Bible, daily reenacts Adam's rebellion against the known will of God. We know what God's will for our life is, but we do not obey it. We cannot obey it. Neither could the apostle Paul (Romans 7:15-25). There is not a single hour in our lives when we perfectly fulfill the will of God in our attitudes, motivations, thoughts, and words.

The Bible puts tremendous emphasis on this problem. Theologians call it "total depravity." However, this term can be misunderstood as meaning that everybody is always as bad as they can be, and that is not the biblical teaching. The Bible teaches that there are degrees of depravity and goodness and therefore degrees of reward and punishment in heaven and hell. In fact, there are degrees of depravity even among demons. Jesus described a demon who was cast out of a man and then went out and found seven other demons *more wicked* than himself" (Matthew 12:45). What the Bible teaches is that since Adam fell no one who has ever lived has been totally free of selfishness in thinking, emotions, attitude, and will. "All have sinned and fall short of the glory of God" (Romans 3:23). As a result, no one can gain merit from God, and no one deserves heaven. Our mind, will, and emotions are all permeated and distorted by sin, and there are hundreds of statements in the Bible on that point. In fact, the minute we say we are not really that bad, we have demonstrated how bad we are.

For years we have admired the goldfish in the aquarium at our home. They glide so gracefully and beautifully through the water. I have often wondered if those fish feel wet, and I have concluded that the answer is no. They are so immersed and conditioned to the water that they do not even know they are in it. Likewise, when you hear people say they are "not so bad," you are hearing people who are so immersed in sin they do not even know it.

Take one look at Jesus Christ in the pages of Holy Scripture, and you will understand. You cannot look into the face of Jesus as He is presented in the Bible and walk away saying you are like Him. The Bible is a mirror that reflects your nature like the mirror that shows the dirt on your face. This Bible is both a mirror to show you what you are and, through the Holy Spirit, the cleansing agent to solve the problem.

We have all sinned, we continue to sin, and we constantly sin. But there is good news.

And the Lord has laid on Him the iniquity of us all.

The Hebrew word translated "has laid" does not mean God took our sins and gently placed them on His beloved Son. The Hebrew verb *hiphgîá* indicates violent contact. The verb often means "to destroy" or "to kill" in the Old Testament (see 1 Samuel 22:18; 1 Kings 22:34). God caused *to strike* upon His Son the iniquity of us all. There was no gentleness at Calvary, and the minute God turned from His Son and made Him to be sin for us, Jesus cried out, "My God, My God, why have You forsaken Me?" (Matthew 27:46; Mark 15:34). There was nothing gentle about that at all.

It was not the Romans who killed Jesus on the cross, though they were the ones who nailed Him there. It certainly was not the

Jews who told the Romans to put Him there. Nor was it Satan, who told the Jews to tell the Romans to put Him there. Genesis 3:15 says that Satan would bruise the heel of the woman's seed (Messiah); through Judas, Satan got Jesus to the cross. But the Bible says the Holy Spirit led Him there. Hebrews 9:14 says,

> How much more shall the blood of Christ, who through the eternal Spirit offered Himself without spot to God, cleanse your conscience from dead works to serve the living God?

But that is not the whole story. Jesus said, "I lay down My life that I may take it again. No one takes it from Me, but I lay it down of Myself. I have power to lay it down, and I have power to take it again" (John 10:17-18). He voluntarily went to the cross.

The ultimate answer to the question of who killed Jesus is here in Isaiah 53: "The LORD has caused the iniquity of us all to fall on Him" (NASB). God the Father caused all of our sins to fall on His Son so that we could be saved. Apart from the death of Christ, nobody in the human race would ever be saved. God so loved the world, He gave His only Son.

Let us never underestimate the stupendous cosmic forces involved in the death of Jesus. His death is the center of all history. It is that toward which all history from eternity past moved like a mighty river, and it is the focus of all history for eternity to come.

We will forever look back on what the Son of God did at the cross that day outside of Jerusalem.

Friend, do you believe what God says really happened on the cross of Calvary, or do you have your own interpretations and theories? No one can guarantee you will survive God's destructive wrath if you come to Him in the Day of Judgment and attempt to explain what His Son did according to theories that are not in harmony with God's guidebook of eternal truth. I recommend God's Word on what happened at Calvary.

***

Dear Father, speak to our hearts this day. Help us to understand the stupendous price Jesus paid for our sin, why He died, what the result was, and how we today before a holy God can enter into the absolute certainty of salvation and eternal life, cleansed through the merit of Jesus and the power of His blood. We pray in Jesus' name. Amen.

4

THE SUBMISSION AND EXALTATION OF CHRIST

Isaiah 53:7-12

The great messianic prophecy in Isaiah 53 concludes with a focus on the submission of Jehovah's Servant in verses 7-9 and His exaltation in verses 10-12.

Submission of Jehovah's Servant

We have seen in this marvelous prophecy the introductory announcement of the mysterious career of the Lord's Servant, the Messiah Jesus, in the last three verses of Isaiah 52. The prophecy itself begins with a view of His rejection by the nation of Israel, which someday will be acknowledged and recognized in deep, humble contrition and repentance. Israel will be converted as a nation in the midst of what the Bible calls the Great Tribulation. A nation will be born in a day (Isaiah 66:8), and all Israel will be saved (Romans 11:26).

The real basis upon which that nation will be saved is the vicarious, substitutionary atonement by the Son of God: the sacrifice of the sinless Servant for the sins of all the world (Isaiah 53:4-6). It is only because of Jesus' sacrifice that anyone can ever be saved; and that includes the nation of Israel, which someday will be God's instrument for world evangelism and indoctrination in the kingdom age, when they will be the teachers of the Gentiles.

The prophecy ends with important insights on the exact circumstances that surrounded Christ's atoning death and the ultimate culmination of that work upon the cross. In verses 7-9, we see the Servant of Jehovah's voluntary submission to death.

> *He was oppressed and He was afflicted, yet He opened not His mouth; He was led as a lamb to the slaughter, and as a sheep before its shearers is silent, so He opened not His mouth. He was taken from prison and from judgment, and who will declare His generation? For He was cut off from the land of the living; for the transgressions of My people He was stricken. And they made His grave with the wicked—but with the rich at His death, because He had done no violence, nor was any deceit in His mouth.* (Isaiah 53:7-9)

Verse 7 explains ever so clearly that the afflictions Jesus suffered were totally voluntary. Notice it tells us twice that in the midst of oppression and affliction, "he opened not his mouth." That statement is often misunderstood by Bible students, who turn to the Gospels and discover certain instances where Jesus did not answer His tormentors' questions. We are told, for example, that when He appeared before Herod the king, who challenged Him over and over again, He said not one word. However, this cannot be the meaning of Isaiah's prophecy, for we discover from other passages in the four Gospels that Jesus had lots of things to say. He opened His mouth frequently to Pontius Pilate and to Caiaphas the high priest to explain to them who He was, the significance of what was happening, and who was the guilty party in His coming death.

The real point of this prophecy is clarified by the analogy given in the middle of verse 7. Look carefully:

> *He was led as a lamb to the slaughter, and as a sheep before its shearers is silent, so He opened not His mouth.* (Isaiah 53:7)

The point Isaiah is making here is that when Palestinian sheep are injured or wounded during shearing, they never utter a single sound of complaint or pain. In the same way, Jesus never complained at the time of His death. He never asked for sympathy and never cried out because of the afflictions being heaped upon Him, as normal, sinful people would do. Everything Jesus did in the time of His affliction was to help people understand what was happening so that they might be warned of the coming judgment that would fall upon the nation because of His crucifixion.

In fact, when He collapsed under the weight of the cross He carried and was relieved by Simon, who carried it for Him in that tragic march to the hill of Calvary, Jesus turned to those women who followed him and said,

> "Do not weep for Me, but weep for yourselves and for your children. For indeed the days are coming in which they will say, 'Blessed are the barren, wombs that never bore, and breasts which never nursed!' Then they will begin 'to say to the mountains, "Fall on us!" and to the

hills, "Cover us!"' For if they do these things in the green wood, what will be done in the dry?" (Luke 23:28-31)

In other words, Jesus was saying if this was their response in a time of blessing, privilege, and healing, what would happen to them when Jerusalem was destroyed by the armies of Rome in AD 70 (see Matthew 24:1-2)?

There is a lesson we can learn from this. When we read the Gospel accounts of the suffering and afflictions of Jesus, we should not feel sorry for Jesus; that is not why He suffered. He did not come to seek our sympathy. God says the proper spiritual response is to feel horribly sorry for ourselves because our sin put Him on the cross, and apart from His atoning work, we would deserve and receive eternal judgment. Jesus is not a tragic figure but God's masterpiece upon the cross of Calvary.

> ### He was taken from prison and from judgment, and who will declare His generation? For He was cut off from the land of the living. (Isaiah 53:8)

What were the exact circumstances of Jesus' death? Look at verse 8. He was snatched away from prison and judgment. When He left planet Earth, it was not amid the praises and thanksgiving of the tens of thousands of people He had taught, healed, and fed. There was not one thank-you from anyone. Even His own disciples abandoned him and fled. The only exception was John, who with Jesus' mother watched in horror from the sidelines (John 19:25-27).

Jesus, the Son of God, lived a perfect and sinless life. Yet when He died at approximately thirty-three years of age, it was in the context of prison and judgment. There were six illegal trials during one night, as He was rushed back and forth from Annas to Caiaphas to Pilate to Herod and back to Pilate to endure false witnesses and lies. What a terrible atmosphere and platform this was for Jesus as He was "cut off from the land of the living."

As far as the Old Testament is concerned, the worst thing that could happen to Jewish people was to be cut off from the land of the living. Their goal was not to get to heaven as quickly as possible but to live on this earth as long as they could, to see their children and grandchildren, to live under their own vine and fig tree in security and physical prosperity with flocks and herds, crops, and orchards, and to enjoy the land God gave to their fathers. For a Jew, to be cut off from the land of the living was the ultimate disaster. And that is exactly what happened to Jesus at the hands of wicked men.

> **For the transgressions of My people He was stricken.**

Many today argue that this prophecy refers only to the nation of Israel and all the afflictions it has suffered through the ages. This is hardly the case. Clearly it is talking about a Person who bore the transgression of Israel. The distinction this prophecy makes between Jesus and the nation is an extremely important one.

Even more amazing is what happened regarding Jesus' burial. Here many Bible versions veil one of the most amazing series of events we can imagine in the providence of God.

> **And they made His grave with the wicked. (Isaiah 53:9).**

The literal translation here is, "They appointed his grave with the wicked" (cf. NASB). The scribes, Sadducees, and Pharisees, who all hated Jesus (and each other, by the way), joined together to wipe out their common enemy, Jesus Christ the Lord. They planned that after His death, he would receive an ignominious, shameful burial.

In all ancient Near Eastern nations, it was understood that the form of a person's burial was the measure of his afterlife. The pharaohs of Egypt spent their entire lives doing almost nothing else but building their tombs. One of those tombs (a pyramid) was built 2800 years before Christ and had 2,500,000 blocks of stone, each of which weighed 5000 pounds. It took thirty years and perhaps 50,000 slaves to build it. I have often thought of an exhausted pharaoh spending his fortune and his life and energy building his tomb and then collapsing in exhaustion of a heart attack into the place he built for himself.

The ancients understood that this life is only the vestibule to a life that goes on forever, and they were obsessed with the question of where they were going to be after they died. In their minds, the kind of tomb one had was a reflection of the kind of afterlife the person could expect. Therefore, when a criminal was executed, it was important that he be given a burial appropriate to his character.

There was a special place just south of the hill of Zion in Jerusalem, a deep ravine called the Valley of the Sons of Hinnom. In Hebrew, it was *Gehenna,* a place where night and day the fires burned as the trash and garbage of that city was heaped into this gigantic pit. That is where the bodies of executed criminals were thrown, and that is exactly what the Jewish leaders planned to do with the dead body of Jesus of Nazareth. They assigned His grave with the wicked, but then occurred one of the most amazing turn of events recorded in the Bible.

… and with the rich at His death

It was amazing how it happened. It is apparent from the Gospels that Pontius Pilate, the governor of Judah, had great contempt for the Jewish leaders who pressured him into ordering the execution of a man he knew was innocent (see John 19:12-16). Pilate decided deep down in his darkened soul that this was the last time these leaders would walk over him. Those leaders made their first mistake when they came to Pilate and demanded that he change the superscription on Jesus' cross from "JESUS OF NAZARETH, THE KING OF THE JEWS" to "He said, 'I am the King of the Jews.'" Pilate refused, telling them, "What I have written, I have written" (John 19:19-22). This was just one little way he could tell them what he thought of them.

Among those watching the horrible events on Mount Calvary were two secret disciples of Jesus: a rich man named Joseph of Arimathea, and Nicodemus, a leader in the Sanhedrin who had come to Jesus by night (see John 3:1-17). They were amazed to see Jesus dismiss His spirit and die only six short hours after He had been crucified (when victims of crucifixion normally languished for days). They rushed to Pilate and begged him for the body of Jesus. Pilate surely knew what the Jewish leaders were planning for the body of this man they hated, and he was pleased to give the body to Jesus' friends instead, undoubtedly relishing the opportunity to reap vengeance on the hated Jewish leaders (John 19:38-42).

The Jews were thwarted in their plot to throw that precious body into the garbage dump of Gehenna. Seven hundred years in advance, it had all been spelled out. Nothing ever happens by accident in this world. God, not chance, is the Ruler and Sovereign of this universe. He had planned the crucifixion of His Son before He created the world. Every part of it was planned. Every event was orchestrated, even the dividing of His garments by the Roman soldiers. Those callous men certainly were not sitting there thumbing through the book of Psalms, saying, "Well, I guess it's time for us to start fulfilling Scripture. Let's cast lots for His garment" (see Psalm 22:18). Neither were they plotting to frustrate God's plan when some unseen force suddenly took them and forced them to cast lots for His garment. God's providence never works that way. Those soldiers voluntarily did what they wanted to do at that moment, and God used their free action as a part of His eternal plan to demonstrate once for all and forever that the combination of human freedom and God's eternal purpose can never be fathomed by finite minds.

After the resurrection and ascension of Jesus, the apostle Peter told thousands of Jews gathered in Jerusalem, "This Man, delivered over by the predetermined plan and foreknowledge of God, you nailed to a cross by the hands of godless men and put Him to death" (Acts 2:23 NASB). Solve that mystery if you can. I have often wondered if Joseph of Arimathea knew he was fulfilling Isaiah 53:9. I cannot help but think that someone must have shown him that verse later on if he had not known about it before. Would you not be amazed to see your life actions depicted hundreds of years in advance in God's prophetic Word?

God prevented the body of Jesus from being thrown into the Valley of Gehenna because "He had done no violence, nor was any deceit in His mouth." He was not a wicked criminal but totally innocent. He was not like the two thieves crucified alongside Him. He was the spotless, holy Lamb of God, and He did not become a sinner while He hung on the cross either. If He had, the atonement would have lost its value. He became sin but not a sinner. He remained absolutely holy and sinless throughout the whole ordeal. He never once had an evil thought or uttered an evil word. That is why God the Father allowed wicked men to go only so far and no more. Here their wicked ways were stopped, and they never touched the body of God's Son again.

The wicked never saw Him again, either, because loving hands took that body and placed it in a tomb "where no one had ever lain before" (Luke 23:53), in the garden of a very wealthy man who had carved this tomb out of solid rock, probably for himself. That was the beginning of the exaltation of Jesus Christ, an exaltation that did not cease until He arrived at the right hand of God the Father in the third heaven above.

Some people have made a drastic error in thinking that after Jesus died and said, "It is finished!" (John 19:30), it really was not finished and that He went down to hell for three days and nights to suffer some more. That is a total error. He did not go to hell to suffer. He went to the place of departed spirits, called *sheol* in Hebrew and *hades* in Greek. There He proclaimed (*kerusso,* 1 Peter 3:19) the defeat of Satan and the release of saints, who in previous centuries, having believed God's Word, were kept in paradise, the place of rest in the upper portion of *sheol/hades*. Those believers were now released by Christ's work upon the cross, to join Him ultimately in His triumphal move to the third heaven. He "led captivity captive" (Ephesians 4:8), and paradise was transferred from below the surface of the earth to the third heaven.

Paul later declared that he was caught *up* to the third heaven, to paradise (2 Corinthians 12:2-4). But as He was dying, Jesus told the thief on the cross next to Him that on that very day he would be with Jesus in paradise (Luke 23:39-43). Upon His death, Jesus went *down* to the heart of the earth (Ephesians 4:9). The Bible says He was in the heart of the earth for three days and three nights, just as Jonah was in the belly of the great fish for three days and three nights (Matthew 12:40). He went down in order to bring God's people out and up. It was a victorious move. While He was physically dead, He was spiritually alive. He was no longer suffering at all.

The burial of Jesus' body in a rich man's tomb was the end of His humiliation and the beginning of His exaltation. With the lone exception of Saul of Tarsus (Paul), who was converted when Jesus appeared to him (Acts 9), no wicked person ever saw Jesus again, though He appeared to a number of believers and disciples after His resurrection.

If the Gospel accounts were fabricated by Jesus' followers, no doubt we would see the resurrected Jesus portrayed as marching right up to Pontius Pilate and saying, "I told you so." Or we would see Him confronting Annas and Caiaphas, the high priest, and condeming their unbelief. But while God used four men—Matthew, Mark, Luke, and John—He is the true Author of the Gospels (2 Peter 1:21). These wicked people did not see Jesus after His resurrection, and those who remain in unbelief will never see Him again until it is too late, namely, at the Second Coming. We see Him only through the eye of faith (Hebrews 11:1).

Exaltation of Jehovah's Servant

The last three verses of Isaiah 53 describe the exaltation of the Messiah. They give us important insight into what really happened at the cross and how it all affects us.

> *Yet it pleased the Lord to bruise Him; He has put Him to grief. When You make His soul an offering for sin, He shall see His seed, He shall prolong His days, and the pleasure of the Lord shall prosper in His hand.* (Isaiah 53:10)

This information on what happened at the cross is very important. Notice that "it pleased the Lord to bruise Him." This means that Jesus was not a helpless victim of hostile circumstances, maneuvered by the hands of wicked men. He was not trapped in a situation over which He had no control. It was God's plan to crush Him; it was not a victory for Satan or the wicked of this world.

That it was God's plan does not mean that God enjoyed it. The Hebrew word here means that it was His will to do it. The pleasure of the Lord has to do with God's will, and God's will often includes very unpleasant experiences. Jesus said, "Not My will, but Yours, be done" (Luke 22:42), and it was the Father's will that He drink to the depths the cup of suffering. God's will for your life may include deep suffering. God does not enjoy it, but He knows that it is best in light of eternity.

The correct reading of the next phrase is "when His soul makes an offering for sin." The Hebrew word for "offering" is *asham,* which literally means "trespass offering." In the Old Testament, there were five different kinds of offerings God told Israel to bring before Him. Each offering told a different story of man's relationship to the holy God. There was the *burnt offering,* representing total dedication. There was the *peace offering,* symbolizing restoration of fellowship with God. And there was the *meal offering,* which represented the dedicated life totally committed to the Lord. There were slightly different aspects and emphases in each case, but these three were what the Old Testament called the sweet-smelling offerings. They were pleasant because they were offered voluntarily out of love for God.

But there were two other offerings that were related to very unpleasant circumstances: the *sin offering* and the *trespass offering.* If a person deliberately sinned against God and His revealed Word, that person had to present a sin offering, which was very costly. If someone was hurt as a result of the sin, a trespass offering also had to be presented to compensate for the loss that was suffered.

Here is how it worked according to the Old Testament law. If you robbed a bank of a thousand dollars but then repented and wanted to make things right, you would have to come to God through His priests in the temple and offer a very valuable animal. The animal's blood would be shed, representing what you deserved to happen to you. Then you would have to restore to the bank what was stolen plus 20 percent. That is, you would have to pay back the

THE FIVE OFFERINGS

(Leviticus 1 – 7)

Voluntary/Sweet Savor Offerings

Offering	Hebrew Term	Requirements	Meaning
Burnt	*'ōlā*	Male bull, sheep, goat, or pigeons – killed and burned on altar	Dedication, complete surrender to God.
Meal	*minḥā*	Fine flour with oil and frankincense given to priest; a portion of it burned on altar	Gratitude and commitment
Peace	*zebaḥ shelāmîn*	Male or female bull, lamb, or goat – killed; entrails burned; other parts eaten by family of one bringing sacrifice	Thanksgiving for restoration of fellowship with God

Mandatory/Guilt Offerings

Offering	Hebrew Term	Requirements	Meaning
Sin	*ḥaṭṭā't*	Bull, goat, lamb, turtledove, or pigeons – killed, blood put on altar; fat burned; carcass burned outside the camp	Forgiveness received through substitutionary sacrifice
Trespass	*'āshām*	Ram – killed and blood sprinkled on altar; fat burned; accompanied by restitution plus 20% to injured party	Restitution/compensation for damages to injured party

thousand dollars you took plus two hundred dollars more to compensate the bank for the inconvenience it had endured.

Jesus offered His soul as a trespass offering. When God sent Jesus to die for you, He paid the whole price, 100 percent, plus the 20 percent extra for those who were inconvenienced by your sin.

Jesus is a bridge from you to heaven that goes all the way to the other side and is not broken at the other end twenty percent short of the goal. Can you imagine going across a magnificent bridge only to be told at the end that you have to jump the rest of the way? You and I would never make it. Thank God, the whole price is paid.

Isaiah wrote that when Jesus, the Lord's Servant, made that sacrifice, three amazing results would follow: (1) "He shall see His seed"; (2) "He shall prolong His days"; and (3) "the pleasure of the Lord shall prosper in His hand."

He shall see His seed.

This has to do with Christ's spiritual children. Jesus explained it in John 12:24.

> Most assuredly, I say to you, unless a grain of wheat falls into the ground and dies, it remains alone; but if it dies, it produces much grain.

You drop the seed into the ground, and out comes a harvest. By virtue of His death, Jesus made it possible for the Holy Spirit to regenerate hundreds of millions of human beings on the merits of Jesus' shed blood. The rabbis who understood this passage in Isaiah 53 simply could not fathom how a man could offer his life as a trespass offering—which involved bloodshed and death—and then have children later. The answer was that Jesus died, rose again, and, through His death, brought into existence spiritual seed.

Psalm 22 affirms this. After describing Christ's crucifixion, the psalmist writes, "A posterity shall serve him" (verse 30). And Hebrews 2:13 quotes Jesus speaking of "the children" God had given Him. Jesus did not have any physical children, and the Jews knew that. But because of the blood He shed, there is no way to count how many children He has. Indeed, He has seen "His seed."

He shall prolong His days.

How can a man prolong his days by dying? The answer is by rising from the dead. Before Jesus rose from the dead, there was not a single person in history who ever rose to immortality. Back in Old Testament times, Elijah and Elisha raised people from the dead, and so did Jesus during His public ministry. But every one of those people died again. They died twice! Surely Lazarus was very disappointed when he came out of the tomb and realized he had a mortal body and must die again.

Jesus is the only person in history who ever rose to immortality—to a resurrected, glorified body, never to die again. Peter said that it was impossible for death to hold Him because He was sinless (Acts 2:24). Jesus said in Revelation 1:18, "I am He who lives, and was dead, and behold, I am alive forevermore." He is going to be around for a long, long time. We must get acquainted with Him for we will never escape Him. And, of course, because He has been raised to immortal life, He will one day raise His children from the dead and give them immortal bodies that will never die again (1 Corinthians 15:20-23, 51-54).

The pleasure of the LORD shall prosper in His hand.

God the Father could entrust into the hands of His Son the eternal destiny of every person who is saved by His work upon the cross. When Jesus said in the Garden of Gethsemane, "Not My will, but Yours, be done" (Luke 22:42), the salvation of all believers was assured, for God's purpose would be accomplished in those hands that submitted to crucifixion.

Note what else happened when Jesus died.

He shall see the labor of His soul, and be satisfied. By His knowledge My righteous Servant shall justify many, for He shall bear their iniquities. (Isaiah 53:11)

Are you satisfied with what Jesus did upon that cross for you? Millions who call themselves Christians are not satisfied. Almost every day of their lives, they worry about whether they are really saved or not. They wonder what more they can do to guarantee their salvation. Some think they must get saved over and over again. Some get rebaptized because they are never sure of where they stand before God. Some feel they need to give money to the church or perform righteous acts in order to help God pay for their sins. All such deeds are totally worthless acts of unbelief. Those who think this way and follow this path are rejecting what God says His Son did for them, namely, that He paid the whole price.

If someone invited you to a magnificent meal and paid the whole price, it would be an insult to insist on paying part of the price yourself. God is jealous for the price He paid for salvation, and He expects you to believe it, accept it, thank Him for it, and live in the light of it.

We know someone who is satisfied with what Jesus did on the cross: Jesus!

He shall see the labor of His soul, and be satisfied.

If He is satisfied, we certainly should be, because He knows more about what His death accomplished than we do. He is fully qualified to be the Substitute for our sins, and that is a marvelous truth to cling to.

By His knowledge My righteous Servant shall justify many, for He shall bear their iniquities.

Jesus knew what He was doing, but no one else did. Isaiah 11:2 says, "The spirit of wisdom and ... knowledge" was upon him. Isaiah 50:4 says that morning by morning God opened His ear to instruct Him and to guide Him. There was not one false move or confusing statement.

John 6:6 makes an amazing comment about Jesus just prior to His miraculous feeding of the five thousand. Here were thousands of people who had left their jobs and homes and come out to see Jesus perform healing miracles in the wilderness. About noontime, Jesus asked His disciples where they could buy food to feed the crowd. At this point, John added a parenthetical comment for which we can all be thankful: "He Himself knew what He would do." Jesus knew what He was going to do, but no one else did. That characterizes His whole work of salvation.

Most of us have very little idea what God is doing at any particular time, but God knows exactly what He is doing; and that is what counts. We are in good hands—the hands of an expert—when we say, "Lord, save me." There is no one under heaven who knows more about how to save sinners than Jesus Christ. With infinite knowledge, He moved step by step to the cross; and when He said, "It is finished!" it was. He knew exactly where He was going, what was happening, and why. He was and is omniscient (all-knowing). He knew what needed to be done; and what He needed to do, He did: He bore our iniquities, paying the penalty for our sins, so that we might be justified, or declared just and righteous, before God.

Now we come to the final statement of the exaltation and glory of this incomparable Savior. Look at the victory He shall experience in the eyes of all intelligent creatures in the universe, humans and angels alike. God the Father speaks:

> *Therefore I will divide Him a portion with the great, and He shall divide the spoil with the strong.* **(Isaiah 53:12)**

Because His beloved Son obeyed Him, fulfilled His will, and paid the price, God will crush all Christ's enemies and turn the spoils of victory completely over to Him. This will be fully acknowledged in the Millennium, but it happened when Jesus said, "It is finished!" Satan's head was crushed, and God's people were redeemed two thousand years ago. It is already settled, but not everyone has seen it yet. Someday every eye will behold the fantastic triumph of Jesus.

But who are the "great" and "strong" with whom Jesus will divide the portion and spoil? If you are a humble believer in Jesus Christ, that is you. God thinks of you as great and strong. You see yourself as weak, small, ignorant, sinful, and unworthy. That is true, of course, and no one knows that better than God. But when He looks at you, He looks at you in Christ. That is the difference. You are "in Christ," and Christ is great and strong even if you and I are not.

The apostle Paul said, "I can do all things through Christ who strengthens me" (Philippians 4:13). The apostle Paul was just like us. He was strong and great because he believed in a strong and great Savior.

When the kingdom dawns, believers will rule and reign with Christ for one thousand years (Revelation 20:4-6). They will rule over kingdoms, cities, and nations. They will replace the present functions of angels—the invisible servants of God—in governing the affairs of the universe (Hebrew 2:5). When that day dawns, there will be no mistaking who God's people are. As 1 John 3:2 says,

> It has not yet been revealed what we shall be, but we know that when He is revealed, we shall be like Him, for we shall see Him as He is.

Our sin nature will be gone, our bodies will be glorified, and we will have authority and power and wisdom in Christ to rule the world with Him for one thousand years and then forever.

But as we bask in the glory of what is coming, let us never forget how we got there. The great prophecy of Isaiah 53 ends with a fourfold reminder of who made it possible and how.

> ***Because He poured out His soul unto death, and He was numbered with the transgressors, and He bore the sin of many, and made intercession for the transgressors.***

The Spirit of God, who wrote this book, will never allow us this side of heaven to forget why we will be in heaven. It is because God's Servant, our Savior, paid for it all. It is the grace of God in Christ Jesus, not our brilliance, strength, or wisdom. It is His work entirely. Humble Christians know where they stand before a holy God.

Are you in God's kingdom? Listen to what Jesus said to Nicodemus, who thought he was: "Unless one is born again, he cannot see the kingdom of God" (John 3:3). There is only one way to be born again, and that is by acknowledging that the blood of Jesus Christ covered our sin forever and that He rose from the dead to prove that sacrifice was accepted by His holy Father. Is He your

Savior? Do you know the message of the gospel? Are you doing everything that can be done to take this message to the ends of the earth?

***

Father, we thank You for this magnificent portion of Your revealed Word. How clear, how startling, and profound are the words the Spirit of God has put together in this great prophecy. Inscribe these words deep into our memory and conscience day by day so that we will be aware of what our Savior has done for us. Transform us by these truths so that we are never the same again but rather think, talk, and act as Christ because we are in Him. Speak to us, Lord, by Your precious Book. We ask it in Jesus' name. Amen.

SCRIPTURE INDEX

Photo Credits

Page 5: "Sign of the Cross" by Johan Hansson at https://www. flickr.com/photos/plastanka/4641312205/ under A Creative Commons Attribution at http://creativecommons.org/ licenses/by/2.0

Page 13: "Before Pilate" by Waiting for the Word at http:// www.flickr.com/photos/waitingfortheword/5612600926/ under A Creative Commons Attribution at http://creative-commons.org/licenses/by/2.0

Page 16: Open Bible, from Whitcomb Ministries, www.whit-combministries.org

Page 21: "Sheep in Israel," adapted from a photo by lehava nazareth Pikiwiki Israel, under a Creative Commons Attribution at http://creativecommons.org/licenses/by/2.5/

Page 25: "Jesus with Children," photograph courtesy of "Behold the Lamb" 2013, Lisa Jennings, director.

Page 37: "Jesus Dies for the World." A picture created from NASA Goddard Space Flight Center image of the earth by Reto Stöckli (visibleearth.nasa. gov) and "Christ Crucified," a painting by Diego Valázquez (1599-1660). Both images are in the public domain.

Page 44: "Crown of Thorns—Bedford Museum" by Simon Speed. Public domain photo.

Page 49: "Crucifixion," photograph courtesy of "Behold the Lamb" 2013, Lisa Jennings, director.

Page 53: "Jesus Fallen under the Cross," photograph courtesy of "Behold the Lamb" 2013, Lisa Jennings, director.

Page 61: "The Five Offerings" chart courtesy of Jarl Waggoner.

Made in the USA
San Bernardino, CA
26 May 2014